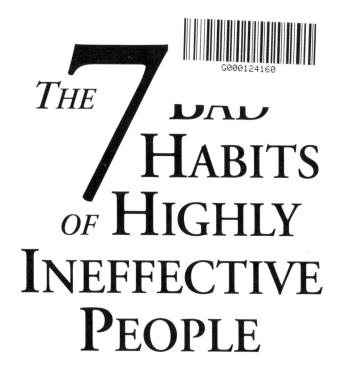

THE 7 BAD HABITS OF HIGHLY INEFFECTIVE PEOPLE

Harness the power of constructive inertia

RICHARD MACDONALD

NEW
HOLLAND

First published in 2003 by
New Holland Publishers (UK) Ltd
London • Cape Town • Sydney • Auckland
www.newhollandpublishers.com

Garfield House, 86–88 Edgware Road
London W2 2EA, United Kingdom

80 McKenzie Street
Cape Town 8001, South Africa

Level 1, Unit 4
Suite 411, 14 Aquatic Drive
Frenchs Forest, NSW 2086, Australia

218 Lake Road
Northcote, Auckland, New Zealand

2 4 6 8 10 9 7 5 3 1

ISBN 1 84330 520 8

Editorial Direction: Rosemary Wilkinson
Designer: Paul Wright
Illustration (page 89): Stephen Dew

Reproduction by Pica Digital, Singapore
Printed and bound by Times Offset (M) Sdn Bhd, Malaysia

DISCLAIMER

Readers tempted to put the philosophy of this work into practice should bear in mind
that it is a work of humour. If any of the tips included herein are actually effective,
this is unintentional, and we apologize. The Publisher and Author would be grateful
to anyone pointing out any true facts or wise advice that may have been incorporated
in error, so that any inadvertent utility may be expunged from future editions.

"Richard Macdonald has written an extremely interesting book. If you persevere beyond the arcane style and wordy introduction you will have access to one of the finest gems of post-modernist thinking. We here at the institute are indebted to Professor Macdonald for daring to put himself outside of the herd."
Dr Maurice Evans, Director, Manhattan Institute for Protocol Reform

"I have followed Dr Macdonald's teachings for most of my adult life and can find no finer guru, teacher and father figure. He has set me free from hero worship and role models.
I just want to be like him, walk like him, talk like him."
Rod Callahan, actor, director, sycophant

"My dearest hope is that Father Macdonald's book does extremely well; so well that he becomes rich enough to pay off his overdraft and loan account. It's about time.
I have given him until the end of the month."
Trevor Holding, Manager, Right Bank plc

"This is a new book which teaches inertia in such a real and positive way that I can hardly wait for the follow up. Simply brilliant. Simply wonderful. Once I had put it down I couldn't pick it up again."
Andira Zedda, author of "Why wait, have chocolate now"

This book is dedicated to Ivan the Terrible who left us all such a legacy of independence, free thinking, swift action, forceful resolve and a complete disregard of the rules.

I couldn't have written this book without the support, research, dedication, hard work and entrepreneur-ship of Bill Gates. Without his help this book could never have been typed, spell chequed, cut and pasted, saved, formatted, printed or emailed.

I am also deeply grateful to:

My brother Bill who strangely disappeared on that desert rally in 1976 and hasn't been seen since

Bill's widow for all sorts of things

My mother and father who taught me never to say never and I never have and never will

My son Jack who has told me a million times not to exaggerate

My son Ned who insists he is a pirate but we all think he's really a private

My son Hal who isn't old enough to know what he wants

CONTENTS

INTRODUCTION

Any intelligent fool can make things bigger and more complex...
It takes a touch of genius – and a lot of courage
to move in the opposite direction.
Albert Einstein (1879–1955)
German-born American theoretical physicist

The world is full of slim, sophisticated, glamorous, famous people. These people are supposed to be perfect. We are supposed to want to be like these people. We too are supposed to want to drive shiny new cars, drink fizzy mineral water and decaffeinated coffee, dine out at good restaurants and only watch cultured movies. We are supposed to read *Hello* magazine and believe it is all true – and want to be like the people in it.

Society expects us to want to improve, want to get fit and not fat, to give up smoking and drinking, to be nice to our children (all of the time for goodness sake), not to have road rage or bad hair days, and we are expected to want to be successful and rich.

Everywhere you look, newspapers, magazines and television channels are full of articles, programmes and adverts telling us how to dress better, get fitter, improve our home and garden, cook better meals, diet more successfully, have better sex, even train our pets better.

But what if we are only human? What if we are not bothered about peeling away the layers of the onion to get to the real us? What if we are happy to remain stuck? What if we want to be dinosaurs? What if we want to lead messy, unhealthy but happy lives? What if we want to slack off and go fishing rather than go to the office? What if we like being shopaholics? What if we don't want a make-over or decking in our garden or MDF in our sitting room? What if we want to be disorganized, forgetful, disrespectful, happy, normal people?

This is the book that gives you permission to be unsuccessful, to be fat, to eat meat and be happy. This is the book for real people who don't want to have their lips glossed, their legs waxed, their personal organizer shined or their car valeted. This is the book for people who want to be relaxed, unsophisticated and very, very normal.

In America recently a new syndrome was announced – *Playboy* magazine syndrome. This is where men are increasingly dissatisfied with their sex life because their real life partners fail to live up to the images in *Playboy* magazine. The fact that the photos in *Playboy* have been retouched, airbrushed, digitally enhanced, manipulated, played around with and generally doctored so the girls have more erect nipples, more dilated pupils, less body hair (if any at all), no blemishes or imperfections, perfect skin colour and tone, perfect pecs and silicone-enhanced breasts means nothing to these men. None of it is real, and yet modern males are shying away from their real life lovers because they fail to match up to the myth they have been sold.

TV chefs always turn out perfect food without dropping any on the floor or burning it. New Age self-help manuals exhort us to face the fear and do it anyway, not to sweat the small stuff, travel a road no one else has wanted to, be okay despite the fact that no one else is, fill our soul with chicken soup. Business books urge us to know smart things, indulge in fast thinking, sell fish, think outside the box, sail into blue sky or water, launch 101 new businesses (mostly on the internet) and find our own cheese. Advertising hoardings insist we have fresh breath, un-smelly armpits, no wrinkles, no cellulite, smooth skin and a perfect shave every time. We are expected to keep pace with all the latest technological innovations, from mobile phones to computers, people carriers to digital cameras, plasma screen televisions to DVD players. God help us if we get caught having last year's model, or last month's – or even last week's. And we are the laughing stock of society if we don't know how to text message, send emails, open attachments, set the video timer, speak jargon or have less than 40 gigabytes.

We are groomed from birth to feel a sense of failure. We will never make the grade because the grade has always been set higher than we can reach. If we only get five exam passes we will be made to feel ashamed because someone else got ten. If we go to college we will be doomed to think we have failed because someone else has got into university. If we do go to university and get a Second, we will be haunted by the fact that someone else got a First with Honours. If we become successful, there will always be someone out there earning more, being better at their job, capturing a more glamorous trophy bride, being seen with a younger and more handsome toy boy. The simple fact is that we can't win. We will never make it if we set our sights on bigger and better. If, instead, we aim for smaller and less, we are at least in with a chance.

This book is about staying small and sleeping at night. It is about getting off the treadmill and refusing to buy the myth. It is about facing up to the reality that we all have spots and blemishes. We have to take on board the fact that we have imperfections and facial hair, as well as nasal hair and body odour. We suffer from weak wills and a lack of confidence. Well, it's OK. We are all a bit like that. It's fine. This book isn't going to tell you to pull your socks up, turn over a new leaf, put your best foot forward, get your nose to the grindstone or put your shoulder to the wheel. This book is going to revolutionize your life by giving you permission to be inadequate, to be second best, to be less than perfect (a whole lot less), to fail, to gracefully not succeed, to give up, cave in, bow out, take early retirement, to achieve nothing, to set your sights realistically low, to have no dreams and no hopes, to be entirely normal and ordinary. In other words to be human. By learning and practising these 7 simple habits you will be more mundane, average and less interesting than you've ever been.

Over the years I have run apathy workshops which weren't that well attended, but now I have put all my teaching in one book so you can learn how to fail in comfort, how to live easily with your inability to use a photo booth without breaking into a cold sweat, understand it is quite normal to fall asleep in front of the television in the evenings, have bad breath occasionally, spill soup down your best shirt/dress and be utterly normal all of the time.

So what are these habits I hear you ask? Here they are in a simple form (we will go into detail afterwards):

- *Habit 1 – Throw your diary away*
- *Habit 2 – Always speak the truth*
- *Habit 3 – Be yourself*
- *Habit 4 – Never say, "No!"*

- *Habit 5 – Practise retrospective budgeting*
- *Habit 6 – Live for yesterday*
- *Habit 7 – Follow your heart*

These are the habits of the ineffective.

By following these few simple habits we can become really, truly ineffective. For ineffective we must read happy, satisfied, nourished. The effective, smug people have ruled for too long. Now it is our turn. It is the time of the meek. But also the unruly, the untidy, the disorganized, the scruffy – people who have hidden in the background for too long. This is the time of the ineffective to rise up and say, "Enough. We don't want any more skinny lattés, we want an old-fashioned cup of tea."

HABIT 1
THROW YOUR DIARY AWAY

*Finish each day and be done with it. You have done what
you could; some blunders and absurdities have crept in;
forget them as soon as you can. Tomorrow is a new day;
you shall begin it serenely and with too high a spirit
to be encumbered with your old nonsense.*

Ralph Waldo Emerson (1803–1882)
American author, poet, philosopher

Are you one of those people who makes lots of lists? Do you keep a diary? Have you got a wall-planner with all your holidays marked in, and every appointment for the year ahead? How about an address book? A personal organizer? Laptop? Palmtop? Answerphone?

The four-stage liberation process

If you answered "Yes" to any of these questions then you may indeed be trapped by list mania. We can all become totally bogged down by the need to make and keep lists to such an extent that we become imprisoned by them instead of liberated by them. It's okay, we all start out from a position of unconscious imprisonment and need help seeing the cage of technology and paperwork we have made for ourselves. Unconscious imprisonment is the first stage of a four-stage liberation process:

1 Unconscious imprisonment – you are trapped and have no idea that this has happened

2 Conscious imprisonment – you are aware you are trapped and resolve to do something about it

3 Conscious freedom – you have liberated yourself but have to work hard not to go back into the cage

4 Unconscious freedom – you have freed yourself and can remain outside the cage, effortlessly and easily

But you may protest, "I need my diary, my mobile phone, my planners, my palmtop, my personal organizer." Do you? Do you really? I doubt it. The Druids – and many other ancient cultures – didn't have any of these things and managed to retain all of their lore, teachings, wisdom and knowledge in their heads. How did they manage this? Quite easily. They evolved a simple rule – if it's important you'll remember it; if it isn't then you don't need it.

Time for improving yourself

If you look at the amount of time you spend making lists, composing emails, sending text messages and keeping a diary up-to-date, you'll quickly realize that you have allowed efficiency to overtake enjoyment.

The magpies of the animal world

We have become the magpies of the animal world – collecting things because they are shiny, not because they will actually help us in any way. We're efficient but we no longer know why.

What I am suggesting isn't too revolutionary – well, not at first anyway. Let's start with a simple exercise. All you have to do is take your address book. Turn to the first page and look at what addresses you have written there. Are there any addresses there that fall into the following categories?

- People you know and visit a lot and therefore know where they live

- People you don't know and are never likely to visit and therefore don't need to know where they live

- People you've never heard of

- People you've heard of but never met and aren't likely to

I'm sure you're way ahead of me here. If you know where they live you needn't have it written down. If you aren't going to visit them why keep a note of their address? If you've never heard of them what were they doing in your address book anyway?

This stuff is so simple I'm surprised no one has thought of it before. Now progress from unconscious imprisonment to conscious imprisonment in one swift movement. Reclaim your integrity. Empower yourself instantly. Throw it away.

Remembering the important things in life

Now, let's have a look at that great ball and chain – the personal organizer. Have you got one? Score 20 points if you haven't. Deduct 20 points if you have. Deduct a further 10 points if you've got one of those really big ones – you know, the ones that are too big to fit into an overcoat pocket. Deduct 50 points if it is red. Deduct a further 50 points if it has any maps in it. Score 100 points if any of the maps are of countries you are never going to visit.

If you have a personal organizer you must now consider why you have such a thing. The rationale behind them is that they organize an address book, diary, appointments and notes all in one handy wallet with lots of space for credit cards, photos and money. On the surface this is all fine. It does indeed organize these things. But isn't organization joining with that ruthless drive for efficiency to make you into a predictable person without spontaneity? Throw it away and try relying on your memory. If an event or an appointment is important you'll remember it. If it isn't important you must question not only why you are writing it down – and investing in a very expensive item in which to do so – but also why you are attending it in the first place.

There is nothing in your personal organizer that isn't already stored in your memory. By writing notes into a pocket book you are duplicating nature and thus wasting time. It is the same with making lists. You already have the list in your head so why bother writing it all down, recording it again?

Now spend a few minutes going through your personal organizer in order to see what you need and what you don't. There is a whole mass of information at the front – on the first page, for example, is the corporate logo of the company who produced it for you – why are you carrying around their advertising? Plus on this page you are expected to list a whole mass of personal details – ideal for the casual thief.

Next is the diary. Usually one or two pages to a day. Why? Chances are you never write in any of it. Chances are it is last year's diary anyway. Throw it away.

Next we come to the alphabetically arranged address section. We've already covered addresses. You only need one or two addresses and these you can easily remember. Throw away the address section.

Ah, the next three sections can almost always be thrown away without looking at them. The Misc. section. Here you are supposed to do what exactly? It is usually just some white paper to make it look important. Throw it away. Next is the Notes. This is identical to the Misc. section – more white paper. Out it goes. Next is the Reference section. Reference to what? This time you get lined white paper to make it look even more important. Toss it in the bin with the rest. Finally, we come to the end section – maps usually. Oh, and some pink or yellow paper, and some graph paper – for what? In the bin it goes.

Now you are left with a leather cover. And what do you intend doing with it now that there is nothing in it? Keep white paper in it for notes? I don't think so. Chuck it. Free yourself.

Setting yourself up for failure

People make shopping lists. Why? Just wait until you are hungry before you go shopping, then you'll know what you want to buy, which will be what you want to eat. By wandering slowly around the supermarket you'll spot things you are short of in your cupboards. We all rely too heavily on such lists. This only increases your need for perfection, which, as we learned earlier, leads to unhappiness, dissatisfaction and stress. You are setting yourself up for disappointment and failure. By relying on lists you are:

- Duplicating what you already know

  Plus you are:
- In danger of losing the list

- In danger of relying too heavily on the list

- In danger of taking the wrong list with you

- In danger of forgetting to put something vital on the list

Remember – and this bit is vitally important – if it isn't written down on your list, you can guarantee it won't get done. By not having a list in the first place you will make sure everything gets done.

So you can see that lists are dangerous. Far better to train your memory to provide the same function. You may need, as an interim measure, before discarding all list-making, to rely on bits of paper, backs of old envelopes, telephone numbers written in indelible ink on your wrist but, after a short time – a month or so – you'll realize that this is more trouble than it's worth and you'll be ready for that final step of doing away with all note-taking, list-making and diary entries. It won't take long for your friends and work colleagues to notice this significant and important change in your lifestyle. Within a few weeks you'll be plagued with people asking for your secret. Give them the good news, so that they too can throw it all away.

Time for change

While you're at it, throw away your watch. Along with our obsession with lists, diaries, appointments, plans and records, is our obsession with time-keeping. We measure the passing of our days in seconds and hours. These tiny divisions of time are entirely man-made and have no reality whatsoever. Who has the right to decide how long a minute is? We casually mention doing things in five minutes time when such a concept is meaningless.

Along with giving up your address book, diary, palm top and personal organizer, you can easily give up wearing a watch. Notice what your colleagues and friends do all the time – yep, look down at their wrist at an object that measures something that isn't real. What on earth do we think we are doing? We set up our entire lives around a concept that is imaginary. We measure our days in units of unreality. Watch-watching leads to stress.

We can consider ourselves pretty pathetic if we can't look out of the window and tell whether it is day or night without having to keep watches about us at all times.

The reality is that the sun comes up each day but that day varies depending on the time of year it is. We get longer days in the summer and shorter ones in the winter. But has anyone ever advocated knocking hours off their watch in the winter or adding them on in the summer? No? I thought not. We divide the day up into equal units no matter what nature and the rest of the universe is doing.

It's much more natural to measure time emotionally rather than mechanically or electronically. So, if you are having a good time, take as much time as you like and if you're not enjoying yourself, move the emotional clock on as quickly as possible.

Let's break it

People say, "If it ain't broke, then don't fix it." I say, "If it ain't broke, then let's break it." By breaking the habit of relying on lists, notebooks, clocks and computers, you can liberate yourself. By using your emotions more and technology less, you learn what it is to be truly human. We have all become trapped by technology. The first Bad Habit of Highly Ineffective People is to free yourself from that trap.

> *If you're going through hell, keep going.*
> **Sir Winston Churchill (1874 – 1965)**
> **British statesman, Prime Minister, author**

Of course this can present problems – any revolutionary system will – and you need to address them in advance if you are to be successfully ineffective. I would be foolish to claim that this is all plain sailing. It won't be, but by being prepared you can work out solutions to any difficulties in advance.

Problem 1: I forget things

Of course you will. This is a new way, a new order and things will be forgotten along the way as your brain wakes up from its long hibernation and starts to play a more active role in your memory power again. During this transition phase it is okay to use short cuts. You can resort to any memory aids you deem appropriate such as mnemonics, knot tying, mental pictures and word association.

Problem 2: I miss appointments

You will at first. If you are breaking the habit of clock watching you are bound to be late some times. But you will also be early at other times which will counteract this.

Problem 3: People tell me that everything I do takes longer
It may also appear to do so to you, initially. Writing letters using a proper pen may seem much more time consuming than typing a letter on a computer, but this is offset by the payback of not having to sit in front of your computer all day trying to work out how to get the address to print in the right place on the envelope.

Problem 4: I feel lost without my technology
Of course you do, at first. We all do. You feel you are standing naked and innocent at the dawn of a new age. You are throwing off the shackles of technology and for a while it feels strange. You disconnect your answerphone and feel real grief because that little red light isn't flashing when you come home any more. These feelings pass quickly and now you have time to focus on the really important things in your life – your loved ones and children. Instead of rushing home to see how many emails or answerphone messages you have got, you will instead rush home to see how many hugs you can get before bedtime.

Overcoming problems
You may need to give your memory a little training to overcome some of these problems. Here are a few exercises to help you:

Exercise 1: Get a laundry basket and fill it with pairs of socks, preferably in an assortment of colours and designs. Now put them in the washing machine and wash on the appropriate cycle. Transfer from the washing machine to the tumble-drier and once this too has finished its programme, put the socks back into their designated drawer. After a week, take out all the socks and pair them up. You will be left with a proportion of odd socks – now try to remember what has happened to all the missing socks.

Exercise 2: Give all the numbers you habitually use a picture to go with them. For instance (and these are just my preferences) 1 is a stick, 2 a swan, 3 a flying bird, 4 a sail boat, 5 a hook, 6 an old man, 7 a golf club, 8 two doughnuts, 9 a magnifying glass and 0 a village pond. Thus if you want to remember a telephone number you translate it into pictures. Suppose you want to remember 340281. This you could render as a flying bird flying over a sail boat which is sailing on the village pond with a swan which is eating two doughnuts with a stick. This is an incredibly effective way of remembering phone numbers or indeed any long number lists. Why not create your own version?

Exercise 3: You can use a very similar method to remember people's names. Instead of jotting them down play visual games with their name. Suppose Mr Carpenter comes to visit and he happens to have red hair and a prominent nose. To remember his name imagine a red hammer banging a nail into his nose. All you need to do is catch a glimpse of that nose and red hair and immediately the name Carpenter will spring to mind. And it won't matter if you don't see him for 20 years – you will remember his name automatically.

Exercise 4: Imagine you are a photographer's assistant. It is your job to develop the films in the darkroom. You can't have a light on in there but you do need to know how much time has elapsed since you put the film into the developer or fixative. You have to be very exact in this. You can't use a light as it would destroy the film, so no torches. Photographers' assistants start out by learning to count seconds exactly in their heads. Initially they use a watch for this – counting and then checking to see how accurate they were. You can do the same. They count each number and insert a word in-between each number – thus one hippopotamus, two hippopotamus, three hippopotamus, four hippopotamus. Within a very short time you will be able to say exactly when a minute has gone past – or five or ten or any other amount come to that. Once you have perfected this skill it is easy not to have to use any form of time-keeping apparatus such as a clock or watch but instead to rely entirely on your own ability to mark the passage of hippopotami in your head.

Exercise 5: You can use your fingers as a way of remembering things.

Use the five fingers on your right hand to mark the days of the week – working ones as you are going to be using them for business appointments – but you could easily adapt this system for weekends, evenings or whatever you so choose.

Use the five fingers on your left hand to divide the day up into five two-hour slots. Thus, your thumb might be 8–10am, your index finger 10–12pm, your middle finger 12–2pm, your ring finger 2–4pm and your little finger 4–6pm. That way, if you have a meeting on Tuesday at 3pm, you can remember right-hand index finger for Tuesday, plus left hand half a ring finger for 3pm. This way you can get at least five appointments a day, five days a week into your personal finger memory, and surely no one needs or wants more than 25 meetings a week to either go to or remember? You could even tie bits of ribbon around the relevant fingers to help you remember at first.

Diaries and lists and watches and computers are for people who have nothing better to do with their time than to make money. We, however, have a whole lot of other things to do apart from being ineffective. Here are a few key points to help you remember this and focus on your new life, free of the clutter of lists and diaries:

• To choose time is to save time

• You can't afford to waste your time making money

• It is later than you think

• Time is a great teacher, but unfortunately it kills all its pupils

---

In this chapter we have learnt:
By throwing away our diary, and our
personal organizer we can liberate
ourselves to total ineffectiveness.
If it is important we will remember it,
if it isn't we shouldn't be doing it.
If it's not made of wood we don't understand it.
Technology makes a monkey out of all of us.

HABIT 2
ALWAYS SPEAK THE TRUTH

When you reach for the stars, you may not quite get them,
but you won't come up with a handful of mud either.
Leo Burnett (1891–1971)
American advertising guru

Why adults feel the need to lie

Let's face it, telling lies isn't good for you. I can't find it in my heart to recommend it. In fact, I would be deserving of litigation if I did. There's no doubt about it, lying is terribly time consuming, takes a lot of effort and puts a great deal of strain on your memory. Also, consider the fact that telling one lie invariably means having to tell more to cover up that first lie. Once you're into serial lying – and who hasn't been at some time? – you are into a whole new ball game requiring great feats of imagination, the ability to think quickly on the spot, ducking, diving, weaving and cunning. It just takes too much work to lie. Tell the truth and you will discover one of the unwritten secrets of real inertia – it is easier to be honest.

Does my bum look big in this?

Let's take one simple scenario. You are getting dressed and you turn to your partner and ask, "Does my bum look big in this/does this tie go with this suit?"

And what do they answer? Invariably the answer will be "No/Yes." What they are doing is not answering the question – not unless your bum genuinely doesn't look big in it or the tie really, really does go with that suit. But let's face it your bum does look big in it – truly enormous – and you know it or you wouldn't be asking, would you? In fact your bum would look big in pretty much anything you managed to squeeze it into, now wouldn't it?

And no, that tie doesn't go with that suit and you know it or you wouldn't be asking either, would you? That tie would look good on a scarecrow if you could find one with as little sartorial taste as you. That tie – which you think makes you look like Elvis Presley/Dean Martin/Ella Fitzgerald – actually makes you look like a prize plum. Stop trying to recapture your lost youth.

The whole point of this is to encourage our partner to lose weight. By constant lying – yeah, you look fine, no, your bum isn't too big – we make them believe they do in fact look fine when it is pretty obvious they need to lose weight. Why buy into their fantasy by lying? Why encourage them to lie to themselves? It makes sense to support them by being honest. It would be much better if we said to them, "Look you really are putting on a lot of weight and need to do something about it," because then they would be encouraged to do something and this will:

- Save their life by stopping them from having a heart attack

- Help them lose weight and improve their self esteem

- Help them look better by wearing looser clothing

- Help us look good as well as we don't want to be seen with a fat or scruffy person

Tell your boss the truth

Lying and being lied to doesn't stop in the dressing room. At work when your boss asks if that report he or she asked for is ready and you know full well it isn't, what do you say? Do you tell the truth, "No, it's not ready. I really couldn't be bothered, it is so boring." No way. You say, "It's not quite complete yet. I'm just putting the finishing touches to it. I wanted it to be absolutely right and need to take a little more time and effort to make it really readable and to make sure all the figures are correct. I'm sure you'll agree it's better to take a little more time and have something really worthwhile rather than rushing and turning out a second rate effort?" (Or something equally sycophantic and false.)

Now, when you deliver a second rate effort several days or weeks past the deadline, you are find yourself having to deal with a very unhappy boss. Your professional reputation will be in tatters and you will have not only let both yourself and your boss down, but also the entire office.

Far better to have told the truth in the first place, thus allowing your boss to place the report in the hands of someone else who would have done it properly. Better for your boss to have a short sharp shock than to have to face disappointment, being let down, and generally messed about. So practise inertia, put your feet up on the desk and tell the truth.

Being the boss

And what if you are the boss? Should you lie to your staff? Never is the highly ineffective answer to that one. They look up to you, respect you, trust you. How do you think they would feel if you lied to them? How would they feel if you got caught lying to them? The answer to these two questions isn't automatically the same. Never lie to the little darlings. They are your underlings and they have to be protected, cosseted, wrapped in cotton wool. You can't do this and lie to them at the same time. So what if they are about to be made redundant? Imagine the karmic implications of lying about such a major event. Better to tell them straight what their fate is, than have them worry needlessly. Once they have been told, they can get on and sign on, find another job, despair, whatever it is they need to do.

It's the same with their work. If it is shoddy, lacklustre, careless, late – tell them. Don't beat about the bush. Let them know straight away. That way they can improve. You can't expect them to get better if you're not on their case. Let them know every tiny detail of where they are falling down on the job and they'll thank you. Watch to see how much time they waste, and tell them. Watch to see how many pens they take home with them, and tell them exactly what you think of them. And don't think for a moment that you'll lose any friends by doing this: on the contrary, you'll grow in their estimation and gain their respect. Staff like a boss who tells it to them straight. We all like to know where we're going wrong. The truth helps everyone.

A few home truths

It's not just bosses and partners we lie to. There is another group of people we really should start being honest with – our relatives.

How often have you driven away from visiting your parents virtually in tears – and all because you bit your tongue and failed to speak out. When your mother had that little dig about your job/partner/lifestyle/dress-sense/the way you bring up your children/where you live/your decorating skills/your car/your new hairstyle, why didn't you say something? Anything?

I know our parents make us angry – they're supposed to or we would never leave home. But there are different sorts of anger and we should learn the difference.

The two kinds of anger

There are two kinds of anger: justifiable and manipulative. Justifiable anger is where you lose your rag because someone has behaved appallingly. It is justifiable because the other person has started it, caused you to be angry, lit the fuse, set the wheels in motion. If they hadn't done what they did you wouldn't have any cause to be angry. Manipulative anger, on the other hand, is where a person uses their anger to get you to do something you don't want to do – it's a form of emotional blackmail. They get angry with you in order to get you to back down or to back off. You are therefore allowed to have justifiable anger if someone uses manipulative anger against you. So tell your mother exactly what you think of all those interfering little comments over the years. Go on, be honest. If not now, when?

You see, it will only help her parenting if you are totally honest with her. Parenting is a difficult enough task without doing it blind, in the dark so to speak. At work you get feedback from your boss, which enables you to improve – you get your regular six-monthly assessments. So too should a parent get a six-monthly assessment.

And who better to do it than you, their offspring? Don't delay. Sit your parents down today and tell them where they are going wrong.

How suppression causes inner turmoil

Suppressing anger, like suppressing any emotion, is bad for you and those around you. By suppressing our anger we increase our stress, adversely affect our health and it can cause inner turmoil which will affect our inner child in a very negative way.

The whole aim of becoming highly ineffective is to live happily, free from excessive strains of any kind, especially those involved in search of status and success. If you look at people who are still bound by these restraints, the ones we are seeking to throw off, you will notice that they are subject to a common loss of honesty, manifested in their relationships with other people. They practise this deceit by:

- Obsequiousness

- Insincerity

- False adulation

- Sycophancy

- Flattery

- Fawning

- Toadying

Suppressed emotions forced
downwards and internalized

Breaking point/
complete loss of control

Rising levels of frustration/loss of self-esteem/
raised levels of rage and bile/
personal contempt for one's inner self

Speaking the truth

We have seen how suppressing anger and other emotions is harmful to our health and inner development, thus we have to do something about this.

The answer is to always speak the truth. By being honest in our dealings with others we will:

- Free ourselves from harmful stress and expunge the inner liar

- Gain respect from others and help them face their own truth

- Feel better about ourselves because we know we are right

- Increase our self-esteem and self-worth

- Become whole and healed

Even though you may want to move forward in your life, you may have one foot on the brakes. In order to be free, we must learn how to let go. By learning to direct our attention, we learn to move in a new direction. Then, we really can release the hurt and the fear that are past. We really can refuse to entertain our old pain. The energy it takes to hang onto the past is holding you back from a new life. What is it you would let go of today?
Mary Manin Morrissey, (1949–)
American author, founder and spiritual leader of
the Living Enrichment Center

Colleagues

Once you have sorted out your relatives and boss you need to be honest with your colleagues. Look, you can choose your friends, you love your family, but colleagues? You don't get to choose them but you have to spend more time with them than with your family and friends. It makes sense then to ensure your colleagues are as nice as possible. The trouble is they may not be. But, if we continue our new habit of always telling the truth, we can change them into much nicer people. If they have bad habits we can tell them without incurring their displeasure, as long as we explain why we are doing it. Tell them that it will help them, improve them, make them better people. They will love you for it.

Being honest doesn't have to mean being cruel. If they are bossy we can tell them without upsetting them, by doing it in a spirit of improvement – theirs not ours. Tell them that honesty is a good, ineffective thing, and no one should be offended by a colleague pointing them in the right direction.

Children and siblings

There is an unwritten rule that we have to put up with stuff from our children and our siblings. Both groups think they can put upon us, take us for granted and all without us saying a word to them about how unreasonable their behaviour is. Now is the time to reverse the old order. Your children are over-demanding and it's time you were honest with them. Tell them how their behaviour offends you and that they really ought to think about leaving home as soon as possible. Wrap their sandwiches in a map, they'll get the message. Give them alphabet spaghetti with the letters arranged to say GO NOW. Sell their pets, toys and bedroom furniture, and then tell them the truth: "Mummy and Daddy want their own space now."

Do the same with your siblings. Tell them the truth. All those years of being teased, bossed around and annoyed are about to end. The memories have festered inside your inner liar and now need purging. Phone them up immediately and tell them you want your ball back and that it was you who stole all that money from the bank during that final Monopoly game. Get it all off your chest in one magnificent moment of anti-peristalsis of truth.

Telling the truth when not asked for your opinion

There is no need to limit yourself only to answering questions honestly. There is nothing to stop you proffering an honest opinion when you feel it is warranted. How often have we spotted someone in the streets and thought to ourselves, "Call the fashion police now! If they could see themselves from behind they wouldn't wear that." Well, now is your chance. Tell them. Go on. Be honest. They deserve it. They are making you look at them in their shell-suit/tight lycra/sandals with white socks on. It is your right to be honest. It is their right to be told they look foolish, badly dressed and inappropriate for the street.

You can take this further. It is so much simpler to tell someone when they have annoyed you, rather than to bottle it up. Bottling it up, as we learned earlier, only leads to disease and ill health. Better to let whoever has upset you know right there and then what you think of them. You don't have to be rude or angry – merely honest. If you feel they have spent too long serving you or their manner has been less than polite, then tell them. Be honest.

And now you have adopted the mantle of honesty, you can move on to the next stage and start telling anyone you disapprove of the truth. This might be people walking slowly, driving erratically or taking too long to use a cash machine. Go right up to them and tell them where they're going wrong.

Other people

This diagram shows how we are not an island and how the key groups around us need to be addressed honesty-wise:

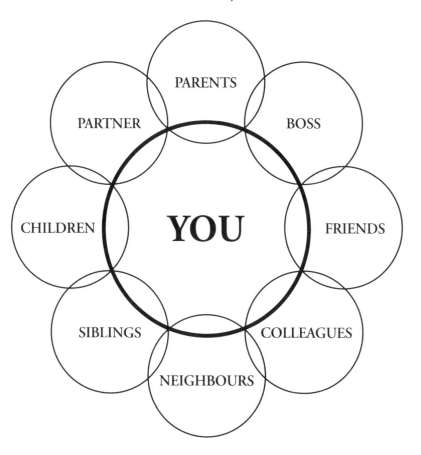

Outside of the major circles are a whole mass of other people – shop assistants, telephone operators, garage mechanics, estate agents, traffic wardens, police officers, tax inspectors, accountants, customers, clients.

Now you have decided to be 'real', you can free yourself of all restraints and tell any of these people who upset you exactly how you feel. Remember, you don't necessarily want them to change their behaviour or actions. All you are doing is expressing how you feel, getting stuff off your chest.

What they choose to do next is entirely up to them. You have been honest with them, expressed your dissatisfaction, purged all those suppressed emotions. You are now free of all that stuff. You have handed it back. You don't have to take responsibility for anything they now feel. You have asserted your rights and are now free to move on. Well done.

Exercises in being honest

Exercise 1: Try looking into a mirror and recognizing what an important person you are. Now, imagine saying to all those people who upset you exactly what you think of them. Look yourself straight in the eye and rehearse what it is you need to say to them.

Exercise 2: Find – in the Yellow Pages – a company that makes shop window mannequins. Buy one. Kit it out in your mother's clothing. Apply your mother's make-up to it and dress it in her favourite wig. Now you can practise saying to her whatever it is you need to. Being a dummy it can't answer back, remind you of when you went to nursery school, slap you, make you eat anything you don't want to, or send you to your room. When you have done this several times, and you feel ready, you can at last be honest with your mother.

Exercise 3: Only by understanding what true dishonesty is can we move into a total honesty space. Practise telling the biggest fibs imaginable for a week or two just to get inside lying. Once you've been there it becomes so much easier to be honest. I did this for a whole month once and found it incredibly helpful.

In this chapter we have learnt:
Honesty is the best policy but insanity is a better defence.
You've got to be honest.
If you can fake that you've got it made.
To find out if someone is honest, ask them.
If they answer, "Yes", you know they're lying.
By speaking your mind you are doing a public service.

HABIT 3
BE YOURSELF

What lies behind us and what lies before us
are small matters compared to what lies within us.
Ralph Waldo Emerson (1803–1882)
American author, poet, philosopher

Everyone out there is going to say or do something to try to change you. Your boss will tell you to be on time. Your partner will tell you to be tidier. Your mother will tell you to sit up straight. The whole world will conspire to make you different. You will be told to "shape up or ship out". Well, they are all wrong. You are lovely just the way you are.

Habit 3 is about coming to terms with the fact that you are the centre of your own universe. If you feel as though you are somewhere at the side, these insights will draw you back to the bull's-eye.

Harnessing constructive inertia is about doing as little as possible, going with the flow, being in the moment. The world out there is full of people chasing dreams and dollars. You stay put and we'll bring it all to you via satellite, the internet, phone shopping, mail order, pizza delivery. There's no need for you to go anywhere, do anything. If you are the centre of that perfect universe it makes sense that everything will revolve around you. You are the best role model for you. Just accept that you are perfect and you don't need to make any effort for anyone.

The role model of nature

We humans have an immense capacity for complicating things. If you take nature as your role model you won't go far wrong. Look at a river and compare it with a canal. A river meanders, winds, follows the contours of the landscape. It doesn't flow uphill or race anywhere. It gently trickles along, minding its own business and doing no one any harm. It is itself. It lives in its own riverness of being. Now look at the canal. It rushes everywhere. It doesn't look very nice. It follows straight lines. It never makes it to the sea and it needs far too much technology – locks and the like – to make it work properly. It is a man-made edifice and, as such, is modern, ugly and efficient. What we want is water being itself, not water being forced into constricted channels. It's the same with any other aspect of nature: it all flows if left alone, and is beautiful, but if we interfere it looks wrong or doesn't work as well – or sometimes even works too efficiently.

If you let your grass grow, you will get wild flowers, wildlife and complete freedom from lawnmowers and the like. If you cut, cut, cut, all you will get is backache, servicing problems with the lawnmower, unnatural stripes and a lawn completely devoid of colour, life and noise (no flowers=no insects=no birds=no sound).

Same with the weather. If you demand sunshine and get rain you'll be disappointed. But, if you are open to whatever is on offer, you'll always be cheerful. There is no such thing as bad weather, only the wrong clothing.

By leaving things as they are supposed to be we get an enriched life. Follow nature and you won't go far wrong.

Chaos is happiness

If you take the really great thinkers, artists, musicians and even politicians (but not estate agents) of the last few centuries, you will quickly notice that they led chaotic lives, socially, emotionally or generally. Take Winston Churchill: he saved the Western world from the dangers of Nazism, but drank like a fish and wore pretty silly red velvet babygrows (as an adult). Einstein couldn't even remember where he had put the hairbrush. Proust never went out without a hot-water bottle strapped to his waist inside his coat, and finally took to his bed for the last 12 years of his life. And you? Perfect. Inert and ineffective. Excellent.

We have seen from Habit 2 (see pages 23–35) that the aim is to eliminate anything stressful, such as goal seeking. Now you can undo the ponytail of your life and really let your hair down. There is nowhere else to go, so you might as well take it easy from now on and enjoy the fruits of your own inactivity. Leave the papers, beer cans, magazines and chocolate boxes lying right where they are. Someone as important as you – the centre of the universe, remember – can always get someone else to clean and tidy up after them.

How we feel about ourselves

If we take the time to look very closely at ourselves we might find a small frightened fish, a half-eaten doughnut or a very small human being with absolutely no idea why they thought they were a fish or partially-eaten confectionery. Are you the fish, the cake or the emotional human? Chances are you are a bit of all three. Some of us may be half-fish/half-cake, others half-cake/half-human. But most of us are a combination of all three and as such are liable to feel out of water, rejected or discarded, barely big enough to reach the barrier at the car wash with our little plastic token. The world is full of people trying to tidy us up, straighten us out, round us off, smooth us down. We have to stand firm and reject such contortionist gymnastics. We want to be inert, ineffective and entirely inappropriate.

Humans have the ability to shift perspective. We can experience the world through our senses. Or we can remove ourselves from our senses and experience the world even less directly. We can think about our life, rather than thinking in our life. We can think about what we think about our life, and we can think about what we think about that. We can shift perceptual positions many times over.

John J. Emerick Jr (1963–)
American expert in neuro-linguistic programming

We want to feel good about ourselves without having to actually do anything. Well, now we can. Now we can harness the power of constructive inertia and by not doing anything at all become superheroes in our imagination. We can become that very centre of our own universe.

So how do we determine whether we are fish, confectionery or human? And what percentage of each? And which is dominant? And how can we change any of this? These are of course entirely symbolic. In no way do I actually think that you are really a fish or a half-eaten doughnut. That would be silly.

The fish symbolizes watery emotionalism, depths of despair, scaling heights, things left unfinished, cold reality and currents and tides.

The doughnut symbolizes sweetness and light, being discarded and cast aside, sadness and stale coffee (the stale coffee represents the enormity of life, space, time and a higher reality or consciousness).

The human being symbolizes growth, maturity, kindness and civilization, evolution and science, art and religion, life and death, pensions and profit, work and play, youth and old age, birth, reincarnation and the infinite void.

We need to look at this list of words and see which area we feel happiest in:

A – wet, cool, emotional, autumn, bitter tasting, leaves, smell of bonfires, man-made fibres, green, metal

B – warm, sweet-tasting, red (and white), sugary, synthetic materials, computers, hot drinks, spring, early mornings

C – dry, savannah, lizards, grey or blue, mandalas, mountains, summer, music, holidays in Norway, zinc, buttercups

If you answered mostly As, you are a combination of fish, bicycle and doughnut. Mostly Bs, a good blend of coffee, human and biscuit. Mostly Cs, then you veer towards the fish/doughnut combination which can be treated with Aloe Vera, massage, intense meditation and appearing in a fly-on-the-wall documentary.

Once you have ascertained your personality type it quickly becomes apparent that we are all a unique blend, a perfect mismatch of types. Once we have built our personality hologram we can move on towards acceptance of the perfect us.

How to integrate our personality type with the truth

This exercise is useful:

Lie in the prone mantis position and clasp your hands above your partner's head. Hold this position until you can't feel your legs any more and then relax. This posture is excellent for building good muscle tone and inducing karmic gratitude.

By now you are perfectly positioned to accept the principle of universal centring. Well done. But there may be a few problems presenting along the way. You may now like to think of them as challenges. Or you may also like to think of them as problems. It's entirely your choice. Either way is identically ineffective and thus fits into our game plan. They are, like you, what they are, and whatever you choose to call them is irrelevant.

Problem 1: Your eyes are bigger than your belly.

It's true. You do seem to want more than you can possibly eat. And it's not just food is it? There seems to be an overall greed about you that pervades all you see. Good. Keep it up. This is a commendation not a criticism. Greed shows the world you are alive and co-operating in the great truths of the modern age – more is best.

Problem 2: Your ego is bigger than your belly.

And quite right too. As someone so recently promoted to centre of the universe, it is only fitting you should be as pleased as Punch and as rejecting of Judy.

Problem 3: Your eyes really are bigger than your belly.

This is a serious medical condition and beyond the scope of this book to correct. Please see a qualified medical practitioner at once.

Now we are getting somewhere. You have accepted the perfection of your own imperfect nature and recognized the centred-ness of your own inane universe. Next you can begin to spread clutter around at random in the mad hope that some of it sticks. This is chaos theory. Effective people are busy clutter clearing. Ineffective people like clutter. We like mess and confusion. We like to be surrounded by disorder and disharmony. We like to boldly go where ch'i refuses to tread. Our yin is as messy as our yang.

Why clutter?

Clutter is a smokescreen for imperfection. If we make conscious clutter, no one will notice our unconscious (almost dead, some might say) inner clutter. Conscious clutter puts obstacles in the way of our partners, preventing them from getting close to our emotional disorder, while giving us a focus other than our navel for contemplation. Therefore our conscious clutter becomes a sort of therapy, just as being tidy becomes clutter clearing or feng shui becomes space clearing – or is it the other way round?

Effectiveness is *how* we achieve, not *what* we achieve. Thus, it is also true that ineffectiveness is what we don't achieve not how we don't achieve it. You may feel tidy, but real freedom comes from conscious cluttering. Make clutter your new friend. Liberally untidy your home, your car, your office. Be cluttersome in your relationships, social life, child rearing. Spread a little clutter wherever you go. This will enable the real you, the perfect you, to emerge from the prison of conformity and tidiness. Remember your new maxim – never throw anything away. You never know when you might need it.

Alternatives

It is a fact of behavioural psychology that exploring anything but the here and now is the professional way to effect personal change. Instead of investigating the adult, it is the child who is analyzed. The route to self-awareness is always devious. In the same way, many people find they can achieve Habit 3 by attempting to be something other than themselves. Try one of these:

- Be someone else. Who will you choose? Always remember it isn't who you know, but whom you know.

- Be nobody at all. This one takes many years of Zen training. This is the ultimate inertia but you aren't ready for it yet. Keep doing nothing, though, and you might make it eventually. By focussing on the target you will ultimately lose sight of the goal.

- Be a rock. Good choice. You don't have to do much but, then again, you might not experience much either.

- Be a hard place. Very similar to the rock option but bigger. Again you may lose out.

Another successful method is to take it step-by-step. When I am conducting my 'Feel the terror and say, "Yes!" all the time, even if you aren't quite sure' seminars I am often asked, "What are the four key stages to setting ourselves free?" I have to answer:

- Believe in yourself – no one else is going to.

- Have a decent night's sleep – no one can be really free if they are tired all the time. Oh, and get a good breakfast while you're at it.

- Practise some form of mind-control – hypnosis, mesmerism, daydreaming.

- Learn to clench your fist and shout, 'Yes, yes, yes!' at appropriate times. (But keep the noise down – the walls are thin and the neighbours are listening.)

Affirming and empowering

Some of my students have expressed concern about the difference between nature and nurture – apart from the spelling that is. I've pointed out to them more times than I care to remember that nature is our potential and nurture is how our parents muck us up. It is that simple. Nature is what we get born with – our basic humanity. Nurture is what gets laid over that – community. Nature is the individual, a result of our genes, inheritance and oranges. Nurture is the social animal, the community spirit, the knees up and the singing, the guitar round the campfire, the fondling in the dark, the smell of the pine trees, the attack of the killer bear.

If we are to Be Ourselves, as opposed to being someone else if that didn't work (see page 43) we need to understand what it is to be human. Being human means being totally out of step with the rest of the animal kingdom. Not many naturalists or evolutionary theorists seem to have noticed this. There are many ways we differ from the rest of the animal kingdom:

- Our need to wear clothes, no matter how ill-fitting or cheap and synthetic, nor if ordered from catalogues. No animal does this.

- Our need to eat a hot meal. Apart from a few barking mad Japanese monkeys who wash sweet potatoes in hot springs, we are the only animal who cooks its food. Not many of us actually like sweet potatoes, which indicates our superiority.

- Smoking. Animals don't do it.

- The ability to do jigsaw puzzles. No animals do them, which means we are smarter – or does it?

- Technology. Apart from another breed of clever monkeys who have been observed poking sticks (if you can class sticks as technology – although judging from the way my computer works most of the time I would be better off with a stick) into ants' nests to get the ants out, which they then eat without cooking them first, we are the only animal who uses technology.

Nature marks us out as animal. Nurture marks us as human. We have risen above the level of the beast and now have laundrettes, cars, mobile phones and fast food. Thus, nurture has liberated us from the animal world. To Be Ourself, we have to take on board these two fundamentally opposed principles. In fact, to Be Ourself, we have to overcome ourselves. We have to turn our back on our animal nature as well as the community aspect. We can't become ourself while we are still under the influence of society. We have been brainwashed, indoctrinated, programmed, taught, instructed and generally conditioned to being whatever it is society demands of us. To break free we have to start defining our own rules and our own codes of ethics and morals. To Be Ourself we have to decide if we are acting according to what has been put on us or what rises from our inner animal nature. It is necessary for us to give in to whatever whims and desires we feel, when we feel them, how we feel them and where we feel them. No longer will we be restrained by social conventions, the law, the unwritten and unspoken rules, or the small print in any contract we have signed. We are now free. In future you will:

- Eat when you are hungry

- Sleep when you are tired

- Scratch your head when the fancy takes you

- Eat in front of the television

- Not go to work ever again if you don't want to

- Wear whatever you want without worrying what Trinny and Susanna might say

Totality is who you are

Now to Be Ourself requires a considerable strength of mind. How do you know you are you? How do you know what you are, let alone who you are? How do you know you weren't created five seconds ago along with all your memories? Self delusion is who we think we are. We have to peel away all the layers, like a stripper, to discover that men and women are different.

Society's requirements for rules and moral codes

Nature, genes, evolution, development, growth, progress

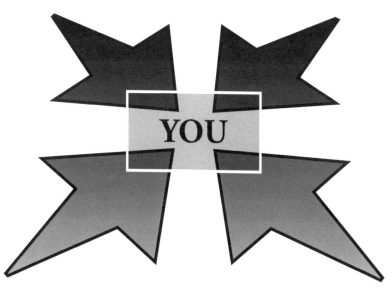

YOU

World politics, international trading regulations, the EU, Tonga, flags of convenience

Universal principles, cosmic laws, black holes, Horse Head Nebular, God, spirit, the ghost in the machine

This has been much written about, but it is surprising how often in my workshops I have to point out the obvious differences:

- Men roll over; women don't

- Men understand fire, metal, danger, guns, speed, parking, remote controls, software; women don't

- Men get flu every winter; women don't

- Men understand the Big Bang theory; women have headaches

- Men are shallow pathetic beasts who don't listen; women know this but do envy that map-reading ability a little bit

Make sure you are going to be the real Yourself – the Anima and not the opposite gender – the Animus. To be the right gender Yourself, you have to get in touch with your Inner Lover. If you are a man and you find your Inner Lover is a woman, then chances are you are straight. If you are a woman and you find your Inner Lover is a man, chances are you also are straight. If you are a man and your Inner Lover turns out to be a dolphin, chances are you have lived too long near or in Sedona. If you are a woman and your Inner Lover is a chocolate bar, chances are you are quite normal.

Once you have made the acquaintance of your Inner Lover you have to welcome them into your life, make love to them (find them some fresh fish for the dolphin-fixated ones among you) and integrate them into your personality. For a man this might mean wearing fishnets and make-up; for a woman buying a handy tool-kit and a couple of cans of beer.

Complete amalgamation

Cosmic integration   Universal assimilation

**Inner and outer Anima and Animus
combined to create the real Yourself**

In this chapter we have learnt:

To attain the centre of the universe of You.

To understand the nirvana of clutter.

That you have been through the several to find the one,
and you have truly believed that
men and women are different.

That you are now ready to accept the five facets
of ineffectiveness:

1. No one can ruin your day without your permission –
unless you let them of course.

2. Others can stop you temporarily, but only you
can do it permanently.

3. Success stops when you do. So don't do anything
and you'll obviously be successful.

4. When your ship comes in... you'll be at the airport.

5. Life is a journey... not a destination.

HABIT 4
NEVER SAY "NO!"

The best things in life are nearest: Breath in your nostrils,
light in your eyes, flowers at your feet, duties at your hand,
the path of right just before you. Then do not grasp at
the stars, but do life's plain, common work as it comes,
certain that daily duties and daily bread are the
sweetest things in life.
Robert Louis Stevenson (1850–1894)
Scottish poet, novelist, essayist

You know how it is, everyone wants you to do something for them. You have so many demands on your time and resources, and you don't want to hurt anyone's feelings. Simple solution? Never say "No!" to anyone. That way you get to keep everyone happy and you get to feel really good about yourself.

"No!" is so negative, whereas "Yes!" is so positive, affirming, empowering, reassuring and authoritative. "No!" is for wimps, for shallow people. "Yes!" is for people who have taken control of their destiny. "Yes!" is for empowered people.

When you say "Yes!" you can over-promise and under-deliver with impunity. People will like you a whole lot more if you just say "Yes!".

So, the next time someone asks you to do something, anything, remember never to say "No!".

Learning to be assertive and say "Yes!"

Remember being a child? All the time you get told, "No! Don't do that!", "No, you can't!", "Of course not", "Be quiet, or I'll give you the back of my hand!"

I'm sure you remember. We are told "No!" so often that it gets ingrained. It may well be too late for you now to do anything about this, and you are destined to go through the rest of your life scared, scarred, wounded, abused and deranged. Tough break. But for your own children it may not be too late – assuming they are not yet teen-aged, of course. If they are teen-aged (or indeed beyond), then they are lost forever to everyone. You can't get them back from dress-in-black, eat-everything-in-the-fridge, can-I-have-some-money zombie land. But if you have tiny tots they might, just might, be redeemable.

Try saying "Yes!" to everything they demand from now on. They deserve it. You will instill confidence, self-esteem, respect and an almost god-like admiration from all your friends. Next time the little darlings want to have a bow and arrow, learn to ride a motor bike or go hang gliding, just stop before you say "No!" and say "Yes!" instead. If they want more pocket money, have friends round to stay for the weekend, not do any chores, fail to feed the bunny – it really isn't your place to thwart them.

You must remember that you are their guardian, not their keeper. One day they will fly the nest, leave the coop. Whether they come back and look after you in your old age will depend entirely on your level of parenting.

If I were to wish for anything, I should not wish for wealth and power, but for the passionate sense of the potential, for the eye which, ever young and ardent, sees the possible. Pleasure disappoints, possibility never. And what wine is so sparkling, what so fragrant, what so intoxicating, as possibility!

Soren Kierkegaard (1813–1855)
Danish philosopher

Research has highlighted this correlation between parental sweetness and returnability of offspring. Professor Golding of Matching University says, "Providing the parent doesn't ever have recourse to the negative word, they will reap a 77% return on childcare maintenance costs during their twilight years."

How we speak to our children is terribly important. You must be aware never to re-inforce negative stereotypes. In the same way, your children are not naughty, they aren't messy, but tidy children doing messy things; they aren't destructive children, but creative children doing destructive things; they aren't violent children, but pacifist children doing violent things; they aren't bed-wetting children, but dry children doing bed-wetting things; they aren't greedy children, but anorexic children doing bulimic things; they aren't setting-fire-to-the house children, but fire-fighting children doing fire-starting things. As such, they should be rewarded, not punished; affirmed, not negated.

Only by affirming your children can you be guaranteed they will look after you well into old age. Additionally, however, you will also be responsible for bringing up neat, orderly, well mannered, holistic, Left wing, pacifist vegetarians. What more could you ask for?

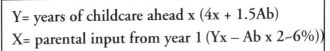

Y= years of childcare ahead x (4x + 1.5Ab)
X= parental input from year 1 (Yx – Ab x 2~6%))

Y = 3cos(7x) – 6sinx   Y= 8cos(7x) – 2sin(4x)

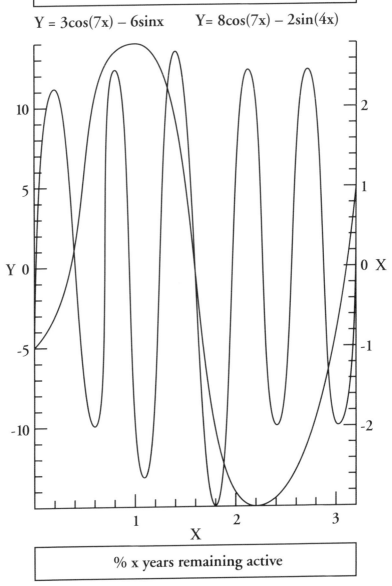

% x years remaining active

You can see from this graph that the kinder you are to your children (the number of times you say "Yes!" x 3), the more likely they are to return home and keep you safe into old age and beyond.

Saying "Yes!" to life

How often do you find yourself turning down exciting experiences, adventures, novel ways of having sex, danger and life-threatening situations, and all because you are afraid? The really smart, ineffective people have learned to feel the fear and wet themselves anyway. This is about letting go, falling down, getting up again. Here are the rules:

- No pain, no gain

- No bleeding, no succeeding

- No strain, no pain

- No hurt, no spurt

- No stitches, no riches

- No agony, no feeling free

- No distress, no success

- No harm, no calm

- No injury, no enlightenment

You have to say "Yes!" and punch the air. To help you practise this, use your children's able assistance. You can incorporate them into any of your positive, life-affirming exercises by playing games with them – chess, football, Monopoly, cards, backgammon, miniature billiards, Trivial Pursuits etc. – and just make sure you win. This shouldn't be too difficult, as long as you use whatever means you have to, in order to make sure it happens.

Remember, your positive, life-affirming exercises are important – much more important than your child's feelings. Once you have cheated and engineered a victory, you can do a couple of laps in triumph, shout, "Na-na-na-na-na!", ruffle their hair and say, "Never mind kiddie-winkles, better luck next time!"

The creator is both detached and committed, free and yet ensnared, concerned but not too much so. If motivation is too strong, the person is blinded; if the objective situation is too tightly structured, the person sees none of its alternative possibilities.
Robert Macleod (1907–1972)
American psychologist

A few days of such practice and you will feel:

- Positively affirmed

- Bigger and bolder than ever

- Full of self-esteem

- Confident and self satisfied

- Smug

Not hurting people's feelings

If the Buddhists are to believed (and I'm not sure I trust them entirely – no one can be that calm or wear such a limited range of colours) we are all one. One *what* we are not told, but we might assume one mind, one heart, one body. If this is true then what we do to each other we are also doing to ourselves. Therefore, if you follow my reasoning, it makes sense to be nice to everyone and that way we are being nice to ourselves. Be kind to another human being and that kindness will rub off on you. This is called Karma, which is a Buddhist word for kismet, which is another word for fate. These words were arrived at entirely by chance. Karma means that what we do comes back to us. If we are kind to everyone and never say "No!" to them, then we are saying "Yes!" to ourselves. This is positive, life-enhancing, empowering and a good investment. Investments can go down as well as up and your house is at risk if you don't meet your mortgage payments. Karma isn't only a good investment, it is also a God investment. God wants you to be kind to other beings which is why we are all vegetarians by birth, pacifists by our fourteenth birthday and all–embracing in our early twenties.

Letting people down

As you have seen, it is better to say "Yes!" to someone and thus over-promise and under-deliver, than to say "No!" and cause rejection, hurt, disappointment. You can always fob them off later with:

- It's all in hand

- I'll make sure it's done by tomorrow

- Leave it with me

If you just say "No!" you have no chance to let them down gently, lightly, or later. Saying "No!" stops the contract, the relationship, there and then. You have cut off all exits and caused deep trauma. Saying "Yes!" gives you the option of lying later to save face, the day, your skin, the situation. But how does this square with Habit 2 – Always Speak The Truth? (see pages 23–35) I hear you ask. The short answer is it doesn't. Look, we are living in the real world here and sometimes things just don't add up. It's pointless to think that things should be fair. They aren't. They never have been since you were at school and your best friend went off with your worst enemy.

Saying "Yes!" in relationships

How many times has your partner asked, "Do you love me?" and how often do we answer, "I think so" or, "Sometimes"? These answers, although accurate, true and precise, can sometimes cause confusion in lesser mortals. It's not that they can't cope with the truth, it's just that they can't cope with ambiguity. It is much better to lie to your partner and say, "Yes!" than to give it to them straight and cause pain and torment. If they then add further questions, such as "And do you love me entirely, completely, utterly?", you can say "Yes!" confident in the knowledge that it will make them happy. Spreading happiness is the name of the game.

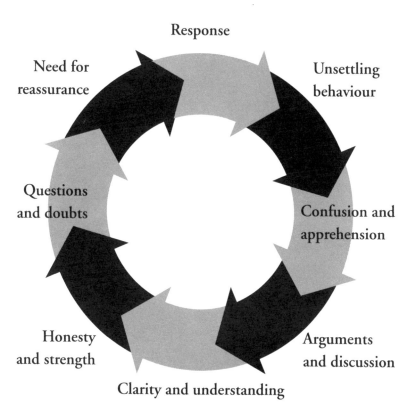

Response

Need for reassurance

Unsettling behaviour

Questions and doubts

Confusion and apprehension

Honesty and strength

Arguments and discussion

Clarity and understanding

You can see from the diagram that it is imperative that we answer with a correct response – "Yes!" – rather than perpetuate the cycle of confusion and doubt. All partners need to have reassurance. They need to feel loved even if they aren't. It is unfair for your own personal feelings to come into this. Your role as a partner is reassurance and thus the only suitable answer is "Yes!". You may wonder: "What if I really don't love this person? What if I can't stand them? What if I am in love with someone else?" It makes no difference. Saying "Yes!" is the only highly ineffective answer.

Obviously the wrong answers to such a question as "Do you love me?" are:

- I suppose so.

- Would it make you feel better if I said yes?

- That depends on what you mean by "love".

- Does it matter?

- Who, me?

And, instead of "Does my bum look big in this?", what if we are asked, "Am I fat?" Any sensible person will say "No!" and leave the room immediately before their partner can ask anything else. If you don't make it out in time, do not answer with any of the following:

- I wouldn't call you fat, but I wouldn't call you thin either.

- Compared to what?

- A little extra weight looks good on you.

- I've seen fatter.

- Could you repeat the question? I was thinking about someone else, someone thinner and better looking.

The last great question is "What are you thinking?" We have to be very careful here. There is only one option: to answer, "I was thinking how lovely you are and how lucky I am to have met you and how warm and intelligent and loving you are", and hope you get away with it. Wrong answers include:

- Sorry, I was miles away, what did you say?

- I was just remembering my ex and how much better in bed they were than you are.

- I was just thinking we could spend a bit more time apart, I think I need my space.

- I was thinking how obnoxious your father is.

- I was wondering what's on TV.

Saying "Yes!" to your children

A lot of parents think that they ought to say "No!" to their children almost out of habit. Unfortunately this stunts their emotional growth. It is much better to say "Yes!" than to say "No!".

Think back and try to remember your own childhood and how often you were made to feel angry merely because you were forbidden to do something due to the fact that your parents were "too busy" to say "Yes!". "Mummy, Daddy, can we go to the circus, please?" I can hear you asking it now and being told, "No! The circus isn't in town." Feeble excuses by feeble people. They could have driven you to a town where the circus was. But, instead, they hid behind their own laziness and made you suffer and feel sad and upset. I bet you cried yourself to sleep that night.

How much better would it have been for them to have said "Yes!" and to have taken you there. You would have been overawed by the sound, the lights, the smell of the greasepaint, the roar of the crowd, the jolly japes of the clowns. This would have inspired you to learn juggling. By now you could have been a street entertainer instead of the boring old thing you are.

Saying "Yes!" no matter what, inspires our children, enables them to springboard themselves into a better, brighter future. By saying "No!" you are condemning them to a future of bleakness and dullness. If they want to go hang-gliding, snowboarding, shoplifting, motorbiking, camping, then let them. They will certainly thank you for it later if they aren't off scuba diving or holidaying in exotic places. Saying "Yes!" is inspiring. Saying "No!" is just annoying to your children. They are only young once. Give them a break.

The *negative rigidity*

Saying "Yes!" keeps us flexible by making us game for whatever is going on around us. Saying "No!" makes us inflexible as it shuts down all opportunity, all challenges, all openings. Saying "Yes!" allows us to encounter new experiences; to gain new knowledge, to develop new skills. Saying "Yes!" keeps us young. In fact, Professor Moriarty of Munchhausen University says, "There is a direct correlation between the number of times we say "Yes!" and life span. In fruit flies and mice we can see evidence of a shortened life span caused by negative responses. The exact number is 17 and we need to bear this in mind in all negotiations with life and with God. There is also evidence that correlates the function of existence that can be worked into the equation if we are bold enough to take the opportunity."

In this chapter we have learnt:

When looking for opportunities, use a torch – it may be dark.
Life is what is coming: it gets fired at you at point blank range and there will be no time to duck.
Success is getting up one more time: all you have to do is get out of bed.
Life has no limitations, except the ones you make.
We don't know who we are until we see what we can do.
Never measure the height of a mountain until you have reached the top. Then you will see how low it was.
How far is far, how high is high? We'll never know until we try.

HABIT 5
PRACTISE RETROSPECTIVE BUDGETING

Man's reach should exceed his grasp, or what's a heaven for?
Robert Browning (1812–1889)
British poet

Recently my computer has been getting slower and slower. I have clogged up its internal workings with new software, out-of-date files, and bits of programs left over after I have deleted things. In general, the processor has become outmoded, outdated and out of memory. The easy and effective thing would have been to phone up for a quote for a replacement but, and this is a big but, I found this impossible to do. The computer shop wanted to know so much stuff about my computer before they could sell me a new one. They said, and I have no reason not to believe them, that they had to know what they were replacing in order to make things better for me.

I, of course, wanted to know how much this was all going to cost me. They couldn't say. They could sell me something but told me, "Trust us, it'll be fine."

That's when I discovered retrospective budgeting. It is a very simple habit to adopt and it instantly brings fun and an element of surprise into your life. No longer do you have to work out how much you've got to spend, or, indeed, what you want to spend. Trust the shop. Let them take it out of your hands. They will work out what it is going to cost you and inform you after they have processed your credit card. You will end up with the best they have to offer. What could be better than this? Imagine having the very best computer possible? Won't your friends and colleagues be envious? They will admire your technical know-how and envy your sophisticated purchasing powers.

So, once you've got your new computer and discovered retrospective budgeting, you can adopt this habit into your everyday life and begin to:

• Have fun with money

• Buy whatever you want

• Shop with complete freedom

Having to limit our spending power has always been such a drag in the past. For too long we have been limited in what we could buy and how much we could spend. Up until now we needed to juggle what we earnt with what we could afford, what our responsibilities were, what we could afford to pay off our credit card each month. This not only limits our spending power but also our emotional horizons. It sets up too many situations where we envy rich people, are jealous of those who have more than us. But they have more stuff because they too have discovered the habit of retrospective budgeting.

Events

Imagine Christmas is coming. In the past, the fun of Christmas has always been offset by knowing that you couldn't afford to splash out as much as you would have liked. You would work out how many presents you had to buy, the turkey and trimmings, the tree and decorations, and there would always be too much Christmas left over after the money was spent. But you were going about it the wrong way. You were calculating the money first and the event second. Wrong. Much better to plan the event first and the money second. The event is what should take precedence but all too often it is the money that occupies our time and attention. Forget the money. With retrospective budgeting you can concentrate on what is really important – the event itself. Cancel the turkey and order a goose instead. Forget a modest tree and get a huge one instead. Forget limiting the kids' presents: invade the toy shop and buy them the best. We'll worry about the details of money later. For now concentrate on the main occasion.

If you ever get into the trap of asking, 'But where's the money coming from?', you are doomed. Spend now and worry later. You usually worry now and don't spend later. At least this way you get your hands on the goods as well as worrying a bit as well.

If all the gold in the world were melted down into a solid cube it
would be about the size of an eight room house.
If a man got possession of all that gold – billions of dollars
worth – he could not buy a friend, character,
peace of mind, clear conscience or a sense of eternity.
Charles F. Bunning (1842–1911) American philosopher

It's your cousin's wedding. You go looking for a dress or suit to wear. In the past you might have thought to yourself, "I have X amount to spend, I'll look at these clothes and hope I can find something that fits me, suits me, is relatively smart, doesn't clash with the shoes I've already got." Wrong. The important thing is to find the right clothes. You want to look stylish, cool, smart. No way do you want to look cheap, shoddy, budgeted. With retrospective budgeting you can go shopping for that magic outfit with complete impunity. Buy what suits you, buy what is smart and comfortable. Forget ready-made; go for tailor-made. Imagine the effect you'll have when you turn up in Armani instead of outlet store polyester. The whole point of dressing up is to look good. You can't look that good on a budget. You will make the grandest entrance you've ever made. At last you'll be the star you always knew you were.

> *Money, it turned out, was exactly like sex, you thought of nothing else if you didn't have it and thought of other things if you did.*
> **James Baldwin (1924–1987) American author**

Retrospective budgeting puts what is important first. You. Why should your life be dictated by what money you have to spend? Instead, it should be controlled by what you want, what you need, how happy you want to be, how ineffective you desire to be. For too long have we laboured under the false premise that you can only have what you can afford. Wrong. There is an old adage: "Borrow ten dollars and you worry; borrow a million dollars and then worry." This is so true. If we earn a little and spend a little we might be effective, but how happy are we? Not very. However, if we earn a little and spend a lot, imagine how brilliant this would be. We could live beyond our means, paint the town red. No longer do we need to hurry on past that expensive jewellery shop with our eyes downcast. Instead, we can step inside and ask for whatever we want. This is total financial freedom. Why should all the good stuff be reserved for the rich. We are all equal, we all deserve the best. Now we can have it. Now we can have whatever we want.

I know, I know. You have questions, you always do.

Is retrospective budgeting for everyone?

Yes, most definitely. If we all do it – spend first and budget afterwards – it won't take long for it to become the norm, to be established and acceptable. For a while you might be viewed as a trend-setter, a bit wild and dangerous, ahead of the crowd, but it won't be long before the herd follows and you'll have to find a new way to stand out, to be freshly ineffective.

Won't I get into debt?

Probably, but who cares? Everyone gets into debt, so why worry? Do you really want to stand out by being a miser? I don't think so. Come on in, the water's fine.

Can I apply retrospective budgeting to all areas of my life?

Yes, of course. Suppose you want to build a new extension, a study or a conservatory. The old-fashioned way is to get an architect to quote, a builder to quote, the decorators to quote. Thus all your plans are limited by money. Much better to just tell them to get on with it according to your plans and bill you when they have finished. This way you'll get what you want – something much better than you can afford. If you limit building work to the money, you'll end up with something that is compromised, too small, badly built, badly designed, poorly painted. It will be fantastic if you can just plan it and get them to build it. You can have big, grand, imposing, palatial, impressive, whatever you want. Imagine how impressed your friends will be when they visit. They always thought you were poor – not at all a spendthrift. And now look at your new house extension. They will look at you in a new light as well as in your new conservatory.

> *Bankruptcy is a legal proceeding in which you put your money*
> *in your pants' pocket and give your coat to your creditors.*
> **Joey Adams (1911–) American comedian, author**

And the whole thing with getting a quote is that it is nothing better than a guess anyway. Why take any notice of it? Why even bother getting one? If there is any guessing going on then your guess is as good as theirs – check out Habit 7 Follow Your Heart (see pages 85–95). You probably know as much as they do, so you are just as qualified in the whole art of guessing. Anyone can do it. Even me, I guess.

How do I persuade my bank manager this is a good idea?

You won't have to. Retrospective budgeting is a conspiracy secret. The bigwigs all know it is happening. They understand and will welcome you into the club with open arms. All you have to do is have the courage to go for it. Bank managers expect you to stay trapped in your old-fashioned prison of financial statements, profit-and-loss and budgets. But once you step outside of that you have declared yourself one of them, a free person, not a number. They will know that you know.

Where's our happiness?

When we are little we are told to study hard so we will pass our exams. Then we will get a better job and earn more money. Once we are earning lots of money we shall be happy. Then one day we wake up and we are retired and our whole life has gone past and we haven't had any fun. "Where's our happiness?" we shout, but it is too late. By setting retrospective budgets we are turning this philosophy on its head. When we get to retirement age we can shout, "Where's our money?" and it will be too late. The banks don't bankrupt old people: there's no point. Nor do they throw you into a debtor's prison. You will have had your happiness all the way along. This is a good habit to get into – have the happiness now and hang the cost. Spend whatever it is you need to achieve that happiness, live a full and enriched life, and worry about the cost later, when you have retired.

Work budgeting

At work we often have to compile budgets. Usually these are based on what money we have to spend, what we spent last year and what we expect to spend this year. Throw it all away. You can't run a business like this. It's ridiculous. What happened last year has been and gone and it ain't coming back. What is going to happen is a mystery. It is shrouded in the mists of the future. How much money you've got is the only fact. This is the one to work with – *ignore*, of course, but work with. No matter how much they say you've got to spend, you can always confidently spend more. What do you think will happen? Do you think they will take any extra out of your wages? Of course not. They aren't allowed to. They will simply give you more. That's it. It really is as simple as that. Spend freely and they will make up any shortfall.

Now you know this simple fact of business management, you can work out what your department actually needs as opposed to what you think it needs based on a limited amount of money. Now you can employ those three extra members of staff you need. Now you can order those new machines you have been dreaming about. Now you can have a more luxurious company car. Now you can choose new office furniture. Isn't it simple? I think you all deserve to have your computers upgraded while you're at it – those old things you're working on are slow and old-fashioned. Ring up for some quotes today; better still, just order them.

In this chapter we have learnt:
That money is a terrible master but an excellent servant.
Why there is so much month left at the end of the money.
That if you marry for money, you will surely earn it.
That having more money does not ensure happiness.
People with ten million dollars are no happier than people with nine million dollars.
The only thing money gives you is the freedom of not worrying about money.

HABIT 6
LIVE FOR YESTERDAY

First they ignore you, then they laugh at you,
then they fight you, then you win.
Mahatma Gandhi (1869–1948)
Indian nationalist and spiritual leader

No matter how grown up we are, we all had a childhood. During this period of enforced, prepubescent development we learnt to walk and talk, play games, go to school, master elementary basics of manners, culture and religion. All in all, life was pretty good. We didn't have to:

- Go to work

- Pay bills

- Drink too much alcohol

- Work with computers

- Wash-up

- Cook meals

- Drive a car

- Repair cars

- Put on make-up

- Wear unsuitable and unfashionable footwear (apart from those black lace-ups)

Anyone looking back might be forgiven for romanticizing the past. But nostalgia isn't what it used to be and dwelling on the past is considered a bad thing. Cheer up, they say. Face the front, they tell us. Look ahead, we hear. But is it necessarily true that the future is all it's cracked up to be? I doubt it. Look at black and white films: no gratuitous sex, no violence, no plot, no decent scripts, no action, no dialogue, no exotic locations, no fancy camera work, no decent budgets, no nudity, but somehow they made you smile, made you cry, moved you to tears and laughter. They were better then, even when they were worse. Looking back might be a better idea than we have been led to believe. Living for yesterday might rescue us from the oblivion of tomorrow.

To look backward for a while is to refresh the eye, to restore it, and to render it the more fit for its prime function of looking forward.
Margaret Fairless Barber (1869–1901) English author

How many times have you longed to slide down the banisters again but been restrained by your dignity, your position? We become moribund with convention and hidebound with standards to such an extent that we forget who we once were and won't be again. We have emotionally turned our backs on our previous selves and become someone new, someone stiffer and more formal, someone older. By reclaiming the past we stand a chance of turning the clock back. It doesn't have to be all looking ahead. There is a chance for us to look back and not regret, not forget.

Most things were better then than they are now – including crime, and statistics. Once statistics have been manipulated they can tell us that 88% of people don't believe them. And another 24% of people don't look ahead. By advocating a return to yesterday it is possible to halt the progress of the future. We don't all have to march forwards like lemmings, blindly going where no one has been before. Turn your back on the future and simply refuse to walk on. If enough of us do it, time can be halted. All it takes is the will-power and the collective imagination of a million like-minded souls. If no one takes that first step backwards then the revolution won't happen and we'll be stuck with evolution. But if enough of us are prepared to stand firm, it is possible.

The 80/20 rule

Looking back is simply a question of pyramid-selling. It's the old 80/20 rule – once 80% of the people believe in something, subscribe to it, have heard of it, then the other 20% fall into line without even having to know about it. Take the case of organic vegetables: once 80% of the population had campaigned for them, the other 20%

simply found themselves buying and eating organic, almost without thinking about it.

So, I hear you ask, why pyramid-selling? Easy. If you tell two people about this wonderful new drive towards turning back time, and they each tell two people the next day, then by the end of the week the entire population of the world will have heard about it – much more than the 80% we need. This is called viral marketing and it works by word-of-mouth very quickly.

Ah, I hear you say, but what happens if someone breaks the chain? What if they are futurists? Well, within the pyramid, there is ample room for manoeuvre. You can have a drop-out rate of approximately 10% and still have total world belief in your ideas by day 9 – pretty impressive, huh?

Obviously there may be a higher or lower drop-out rate and your figures will have to be adjusted accordingly. This is quite easy to do. Follow the formulae of multiplying your daily figure by itself to infinity less the drop-out rate and you will eventually arrive at a total figure for world population give or take your drop-out rate.

False memory syndrome

It is true that recently there has been widespread abuse amongst anti-futurists like myself. Some have been claiming a rosier past than we have otherwise been led to believe – or expected! Others have been deliberately rewriting their childhood to include happy memories, cuddlesome relatives, joyous days out, benign Christmases and celebratory days out. We must, of course, consider why anyone would want to do this. Having a happy childhood isn't a prerequisite of being an anti-futurist so that can't be the reason. It is possible that certain people are creating these false memory syndromes to make themselves more interesting. They hope that by having had a happy childhood, people will be more sympathetic to them. We know that futurists like to dwell on an unhappy past in order to make the future look good. Thus we reason that the world is divided into three main groups – or orders – of people:

- Futurists

- Anti-futurists

- In-betweeners

This last group – or order – is by far the most non-numerous. Futurists do account for 97% of the population which is around nearly all of everybody. Anti-futurists are in a minority (but a very powerful one seeing as how I am in it).

Living in the past on a day-by-day basis

We have to create the habit of saying:

- "Yes, but it was better before."

- "I remember when…"

- "You youngsters know nothing. I…"

- "I've lived through a war, so…"

Whatever the situation we can prove categorically that it was done better before. Transport ran more smoothly in the past. Couples got on better. Disease wasn't so virulent or destructive. Wars were cleaner and over more quickly. History was kinder and less biased. Food tasted better. Children were better behaved. In general, everything was better. By living in the past we return to that glorious idyll of yesteryear. We can bask comfortably in the knowledge that our ancestors were a cleverer bunch than we are. Their lives were simpler, less messy, stress-free and harmonious. Today we have become stressed, indolent and complicated. A return to yesterday frees us from all the troubles a modern society brings to us.

That is the land of lost content, I see it shining plain,
the happy highways where I went and cannot come again.
A. E. Housman (1859–1936) British poet, scholar

Living in the past gives us enormous benefits in our relationships. We need to constantly strive for perfection in our partner and nothing helps them better than knowing they aren't as good as any previous partners we have had. It keeps them on their toes. Just reminding them that your ex did things better is usually enough. If it isn't, then point out that they too will be praised to the heavens when they have ceased to be your partner and have been relegated to the ranks of your exes.

Better friends then

You can remind your friends that the friends you had when you were at school were more loyal, nicer, kinder, and stayed in touch more often. Your friends will be delighted with your honesty and strive ever harder for that perfection we seek in all things. They will be glad of the opportunity to improve. Again you can remind them that they will be elevated to the ranks of perfect friends immediately when they have ceased to be your friends by merest dint of your philosophy that everything that happened before is better than what is happening now and infinitely better than anything that can happen in the future.

Cute kids

No matter what stage your children are going through they will never be so delightful, so cute, so cuddlesome as they were when they were younger. If they do well in exams, simply remind them how much brighter they were when they were younger and how they have let their standards slip. They will try harder knowing that they have a very high level to maintain.

The other place was better

At work you can tell people that the place you worked at before was busier, the staff friendlier, the hours shorter, the pay better and the boss much nicer. It doesn't hurt to tell the boss this as it can often help them pull their socks up and become much nicer themselves. Colleagues also appreciate the fact that they too can improve and will be pleased that you have told them how to.

Is this as good as it was in the past?

By living in the past we enrich our lives, empower ourselves in a very real and positive way, and have a constant set of reference points – standards if you like – to refer to. This helps us to touch base with perfection: everything we have, experience, buy or want, can be checked back, as we ask, "Is this as good as it was in the past?" Of course the answer is always "No!" but it helps us make up our mind and to see how quality has slipped. There are a few important rules to bear in mind:

- This isn't as good as the last time I did it.

- I remember this as being better.

- Things can only get worse.

- There is nothing up ahead that is half as good as what is behind.

- Time hurts everything.

- One day we'll look back and laugh.

The relationship between the past and the future

When we look back we might be tempted into thinking there is less past than there is future. But if you think about it for a moment there is exactly the same amount of time behind us as there is in front of us. We have all been born exactly in the middle of time with the same amount stretching backwards and forwards in both directions. If we are to take into account third and fourth dimensions there might well be the same amount stretching up and down from us as well.

If we see ourselves as surrounded by time and space it makes sense to pay as much attention to the past as to the future. Just because

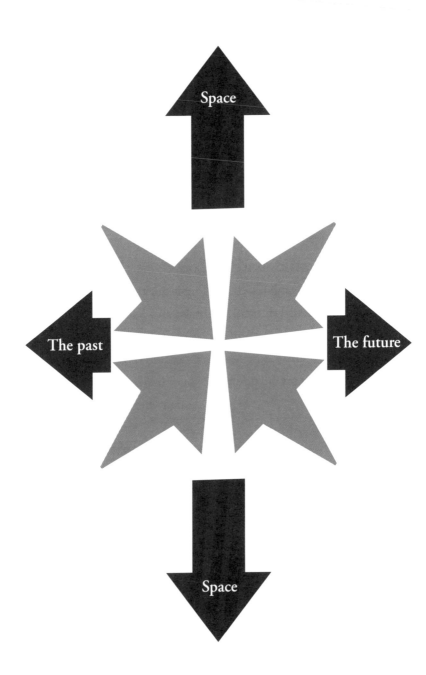

we think we can't access the past, it doesn't mean it is gone and forgotten. All of our formative years lie in the past and we can rewrite our memories to improve our sense of self-worth and esteem. We can likewise access the future, but only if we are patient.

Accessing the past

We have this false notion that the future holds everything that is going to change our life – to make it more interesting, more fulfilled, more satisfying. However, if we examine the truth around us, we will discover it is to the past that we really owe our loyalty and gratitude.

Here are a few examples. Every book you have read was written in the past. There has never been a case of anyone in the future writing anything that has ever been of any use to us whatsoever. Think about that for a moment. Think of all the billions and billions of people to come, and realize that not one of them will think it worth their time to offer you any advice or help or useful hints and tips as to how you can do better in this life. Now think of all the people in the past who have offered to help. Even this book you are reading at this very moment is a dedicated document from the past. It was written in the past, printed, produced and designed in the past. You bought it in the past and the second you have finished reading it, it will be in the past. Now how much have you read from the future? Not a single word. That's how much the futurists think of you.

Another example is food. Every scrap was grown, harvested and then sold to you by the supermarkets in the past. Farmers of the future? They don't care if you live or die. They don't grow anything for you. The same is true of your clothes, everything in your house, the TV you watch, the car you drive, your holidays.

The power of then

Increasingly we are told to "live in the moment", that "now" has a certain power, that being "here and now" is important. However, these philosophies are impossible. The second of "now" is gone and past before we have grasped it. Scientists used to think that time happened in individual tiny droplets of about 0.0000000000003 of a second. But recent research, using massive telescopes and measuring the rate that light reaches us from the most distant stars we can see, proves that time is in fact a continuous stream and not divided up. Trying to grasp a single moment such as "now" is impossible as the stream of time has already passed us by before we can achieve this.

If we can't grasp the "now", we can at least grasp the "then". This is much more achievable and helpful. "Then" has tremendous power as we can really begin to be ineffective by concentrating on the past. Who wants to be successful and important, anyway, if it requires us to live in a totally false time zone such as the future?

Other benefits

By living in the past we can spend as much time as we want enjoying experiences we have previously enjoyed. If we live in the future these experiences are gone before we have really even noticed them; and once gone they cannot be recaptured, except by us nostalgists. We can replay anything we want that was previously experienced. This means we no longer need to rely on others to provide us with satisfaction or have to wait for anyone else to give us anything we need. We have everything we could possibly want already neatly locked up in our memory banks. This freedom from anyone else, this new self-reliance, is liberating in ways we can only hint at.

Not only do we have all these memories stored away but we can also modify them to improve them if we so desire. How much of the future can we do this with? None, of course. This makes the past safe. We can safely go back knowing that we can edit, erase, improve, recast, fast forward and freeze frame any part of our past. The future on the other hand is random, unpredictable, dangerous, unknown, unplanned, unprepared for, scary, volatile and uncoordinated.

What lies ahead

The past is our safety zone, the future our danger. You can see why it makes so much sense to turn our backs on the future and live for yesterday. Ahead lies ageing and decay, illness and decline. The past contains birth and youth, health and energy, fun and pleasure, vitality and enthusiasm. We were better off in the past, we shall be worse off in the future.

We are told to strive for perfection – when? In the future, of course. We are encouraged to improve – when? In the future, of course. We are exhorted to wear new fashions – when? You guessed it, in the future. We are urged to lose weight, get fit, look younger – all in the future.

New Year's Resolutions are always for the year ahead. Why? Why not decide to give up something for the year that has gone? Ah, that would be too easy, wouldn't it? That would require almost no effort at all. And the one thing the futurists want us to do is be effective, successful, productive, lean and mean. Well we don't want that. We want to be lazy and indulgent, pleasure seeking and happy. Never mind keep fit, we want keep fat. By living in the past we can hold on to all of our memories of being slim and young and thus not have to worry about any of that stuff any more. By living in the past we have already achieved everything we could possibly want. Brilliant.

In this chapter we have learnt:
That time and tide wait for no one.

Time weighs heavy.

There is nothing that looks better than looking back.

HABIT 7
FOLLOW YOUR HEART

Nothing in the world can take the place of persistence.
Talent will not; nothing is more common than
unsuccessful men with talent. Genius will not;
un-rewarded genius is almost a proverb.
Education will not; the world is full of educated derelicts.
Persistence and determination alone are omnipotent.
The slogan, "Press on", has solved and always
will solve the problems of the human race.
Calvin Coolidge (1872–1933)
American President (1923–1929)

Have you noticed how facts always seem to muddy the issue? You are an intuitive, instinctive creature of the universe. You know stuff. Listen to what your heart says and know it is true. While you remain grounded in facts you will never be truly ineffective. How could you be? By living in cloud-cuckoo-land you can liberate yourself from having to deal in reality, trade facts or earn a living. By following your heart you can wallow in sequinned bath robes all day long, impress your friends with your counselling skills, attract the perfect partner and start your own business practising amateur psychology, reading tarot cards, doing charts or running a wholefood, organic, vegetarian café. You could be a healer, a storyteller, a fundamentalist, born-again New Ager. All you have to do is develop the habit of following your heart. But how to do this?

A few lessons

Easy. We shall have to work through a few lessons but this is a habit that anyone can learn by unlearning, by not learning. It's a trick of the light, an art form, a cunning deception played on your mind to deceive it into standing back to allow that inner voice to be heard.

Lesson 1: Forget the facts. We all think facts have it, that they are the reality and that they win out over instinctive knowledge. But how true is this? Look at someone like Darwin. He knew nothing until one day he got an intuitive idea, listened to his heart and his Theory of Evolution was born. But until he gave birth to it, it didn't exist. It wasn't a fact until he said it was. Then everyone accepted it and went around saying, "Golly, isn't he clever? He knows facts about evolution we didn't even know we didn't know." Now take the Big Bang theory. How accurate is this? Both as a theory and as a bang? There is no way of proving it. There is no way of disproving it. Scientists say the universe began with a Big Bang. Fine. But do they tell us how big? How colourful? What sort of explosion was it? These things they fail to tell us. Now sit quietly in a darkened room and ponder these questions. Inside your head, in the darkness, you will see a tiny flash, a firework going off. This is your instinctive knowledge of the start of the universe. This is your heart telling you stuff your mind couldn't even begin to dream of. This exercise works for every human being alive. If we ponder the start of the universe in a darkened room and concentrate on the Big Bang we will see it in our mind's eye. We already have access to information that no scientist could ever give us.

Lesson 2: Make a banana milkshake. If you don't like banana make a strawberry one. Again, sit in a darkened room and sip it slowly. Wear a blindfold. Now tell me what it is you can taste. How tasty is it? Where does this taste come from? What chemicals make this taste? The scientists could tell you the chemical formulae of this taste but they couldn't describe what it is you are tasting. We taste with our heart if you like. Our mind provides no part in this process. Taste is an instinctive thing – we can all do it without any training.

Lesson 3: The nature of God. Pretend for a moment you are the wisest person alive in the universe. I come to you and ask, "What is the nature of God?" You can answer anything you like. Just say the first thing that comes into your head. Don't think about it for a single second. Whatever you say is the truth. This is the actual reality of God, because whatever you say is true. God is everything, everywhere and everywhen. Therefore, whatever you say will incorporate some aspect of God. You will have accurately described God without ever having met him. You will also have been able to put into words simply and easily that which hermits, priests, religious leaders and poets have struggled with for thousands of years. In an instant you have indeed become the wisest person in the entire universe.

Lesson 4: This is the last one, I promise. I was going to give you lots more but my heart just spoke clearly to me and said to pack it in as I might overload you with new experiences. So, last exercise. Back to the darkened room. Sit comfortably but don't fall asleep. Well, you can if you are very tired, and resume this later when refreshed. Now close your eyes and listen. In the depths of your mind you will hear a voice. This voice may harry you: "What are you doing, doing this?" It may suggest you might be better off somewhere else, doing something else. It might suggest you have left the gas on even though you know full well your home is entirely electric. What is this voice? Where does it come from? No one knows. It has been suggested it is your own mind. If this is true, whose is the voice that argues with it? Is that your own mind as well? Are there two of them? Are you ill? I don't think so, because while you listen to these two arguing you can hear another one listening in to the first two who are still arguing. This third voice is your heart. Listen long enough and hard enough, and it will speak to you.

Good. And relax. Now comes the practical stuff. First, it might be helpful to see how this whole mind, id, ego, heart stuff works visually.

Clarifying our terms

It might be useful to just clarify what we mean by some of these terms before seeing the diagram. Ego – mannerisms and personality: this is our basic character; how we go about our everyday life; what others see in us; how we move and assume and feel and sleep; what newspaper we read; what yogurt we buy; where we do our shopping; where we go on holiday. Id – basic instructs and sexual drive: this is how we make love; what positions we choose; whether we are gay or just happy; how many times a night we need to get up to visit the bathroom. Heart – emotions and displacement activities: this is who and why we love; our childhood sweethearts and how we had our first bumbling sexual encounters which led us to formulate our sexual experiences. Super-id – intelligence and intellect: how we think.

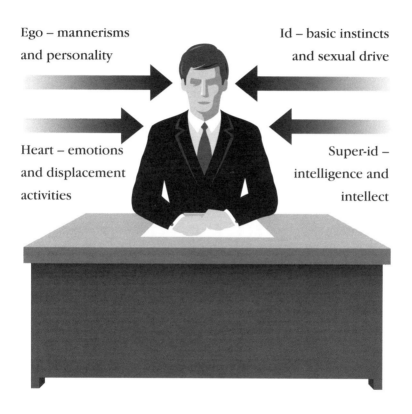

Ego – mannerisms and personality

Id – basic instincts and sexual drive

Heart – emotions and displacement activities

Super-id – intelligence and intellect

We are made of many layers – a bit like an onion really

You can see that we are all made up of many layers, some imposed on us by our upbringing. To follow our heart we have to strip away these imposed layers and learn to trust our "higher self". This higher self is a cosmic part of us. We can trust it as it only has our best interests at heart. There is nothing we encounter in our lives that our higher self hasn't already set up for us as a series of life lessons. We might think we are just unhappy, but it is actually our heart that has deliberately caused this to be so we can learn from it. Learn, grow and move on.

Listening to our heart

Before we can listen to our heart, we have to find out how to listen. We do this by channelling our focus down inside of ourselves to our heart chakra. If you put your hand on your chest and literally pull your hand down towards your solar plexus, you will draw the strings of your heart chakra shut. This closes you down and stops your heart from speaking. It is very effective. However, we want to be ineffective, to throw all caution to the wind and become free, creating a literal heart space. We do this by opening the strings of the heart chakra.

Sit cross-legged and clutch your solar plexus. Open your hand and feel your heart open as you do so. Bring your hand up and out in a universal sign of peace and offering. As you do this you will feel your heart open, blossom, sing.

The sensual and spiritual are linked together by a mysterious bond, sensed by our emotions, though hidden from our eyes. To this double nature of the visible and invisible world — to the profound longing for the latter, coupled with the feeling of the sweet necessity for the former, we owe all sound and logical systems of philosophy, truly based on the immutable principles of our nature, just as from the same source arise the most senseless enthusiasms.

Karl Wilhelm Von Humboldt (1767–1835)

German statesman, philologist

Beware of listening to someone else's heart

It does happen. We are sitting quietly in our meditation room minding our own business, when we hear a voice loud and clear within the space inside of our own mind.

It might say, "Have doughnuts," or "Calm the wildebeest." These thoughts/voices/sounds could be our heart speaking to us, but they are not. We have accidentally tuned into the cosmic phone and are listening to someone else's heart. We have got a cosmic wrong number. We shall have to hang up and dial again when the line has been cleared. The best way to do this is to get up and stand with your hands by your side, fists tightly clenched. Open your mouth as wide as you can and make the universal hanging-up sound: "Ohmn". This sound clears the cosmic energy, thus giving the other heart a chance to get off the line before allowing your heart to open up and speak clearly to you, as normal.

On other occasions, you might even get another heart speaking to you in a completely foreign language.

It might say, "*Fleeder mine got, Einerrustrat, nein, nein, profungbeirstenin!*" or something to that effect. Ignore it. It is annoying but not harmful.

The demons in your head

There aren't any. Ignore anyone who says you are playing with the devil's work. Open your chakra in front of them and shame them with your openness and honesty. They have invariably seen too many films which feature demonic possession, have recently given up smoking and are ready to bite the heads off live rats, or were denied access to fantasy novels as a child.

The demons in someone else's head

It does happen very occasionally that someone else's demons may speak to you via someone else's heart. We call this a double crossed line and invariably they speak to you in double Dutch or gobbledygook. Switch off both phones and use email instead.

Being patronizing

Once you have perfected the open heart chakra movement, then practise it as often as you can. It is especially appealing to do it as you speak to others. Let them know you are working with the heart chakra. Let them see the heart space opening your eyes. Let them see how loving, forgiving and patronizing you have become. This last one is important because we often think it means being condescending to others, but it doesn't: it actually means acting like a patron – a wealthy benefactor. And that is exactly what you have become. You now have a wealth of heart love and can bestow these riches on others. They can receive your bounteous gifts and they too might grow and shine as you are.

Once you are at this stage, you are ready to begin living in your heart-space. You have become a shining being of light. No longer will the troubles and woes of the world drag you down, for you can see through them all, and see the petty reality behind them. Now you are free to follow your heart.

Wake each day and untie the strings of your heart chakra. Lie in bed until you feel ready to face the day. There is no rush. There is only perfect peace in this, your heart space. When you are ready you can get up and break your fast with a little low fat carrot and apple juice (organic of course), or a large, greasy fry-up.

Are you giving or taking?

The day is now yours to do with as you want. If you are obliged to go to work you must think long and hard about the karmic implications of what you do. Is what you do sustaining or depleting the planet's reserves? Are you giving or taking? Are you part of the problem or part of the solution? Are you helping and healing, or hurting and hating?

From now on, every action, every movement, every word spoken should be accompanied by your hand gesture showing that you are permanently opening your heart chakra. (Unless, of course, you feel threatened or intimidated by anyone else who fails to join you in this heart revolution.)

Indeed, there are some – gross beings who are known as new souls – unlike you, who has been around so many times that this is probably your last manifestation as a mortal soul and you are ready for the great trip to paradise – who won't understand. In fact they may be positively hostile. A quick shutting-down gesture is usually enough to silence them. When you are alone again or amongst friends, you can reopen the strings.

Going back over your life

If you go back over your life you will see that at times you have been faced with choices, perhaps difficult decisions, and have had to make a number of turns at various crossroads. How did you go about making such a choice? Did you weigh up the pros and cons? Seek advice? Ask for divine guidance? Talk to friends? All of these? None of these? And how did the choice turn out? The statistics make for interesting reading:

	Professional advice	Advice from friends	Random choice– sticking a pin in	Following the heart
Success rating	43%	24%	50%	100%
Fun value	21%	59%	94%	87%
Satisfaction levels	42%	23%	4%	92%

From this we can see that following your heart has a much higher success rating, satisfaction level and only gets let down slightly on the fun factor. Obviously looking at statistics can be helpful but you should ask your heart whether this information is of any value.

Get a job

Let's take a common scenario. You are going for an interview. I know it is a fairly remote possibility, but it might just crop up. How do you determine what to wear? The standard advice is to dress appropriately. But what does this mean? Listen to your heart. Wear whatever you feel is best for you. If everyone else is wearing a smart suit, but you feel like wearing soft, flowing robes of purple, then do so. They will be amazed at your confidence, your dedication, your openness.

Having arrived at the interview, it is considered correct to look cheerful, sit upright, ask the right questions, appear interested and alert. Forget it. You need to clear the room properly. You couldn't possibly be interviewed in a room full of negative energy. Space clearing is an important part of any interview and you will have to do it immediately. Before they go through your CV or ask any questions about your experience, qualifications, background, suitability, get in first and insist the room is recharged with positive energy. Go to the four quadrants – north, south, east and west, and light a stick of incense in each corner – frankincense is best but a little ylang ylang will do. Clear the negative energy by waving the smoke and chanting an appropriate space clearing chant:

Om, Om, clear this space
Om, Om, out darkness, out negativity
Om, Om, fill this void
Love and light, light and love

Once this is done you can sprinkle a little water from a holy well in each corner. This will ground any fresh positive energy keeping it balanced and full. Now you are ready for your interview. Good luck.

In this chapter we have learnt:
The spiritual is the parent of the practical.
Your treasure house is within; it contains all you need.
Spirit is matter seen in a stronger light.
Physical strength is measured by what we can carry;
spiritual by what we can bear.

CONCLUSION

Is that enough? Are you ready to be ineffective now? Are you ready to be the problem and not the solution? I certainly hope so. For centuries this world has been screwed up by people trying to be successful, to set us all in order and neatness. Well, now is the time to rebel, to reclaim our messiness, our disorganization, our chaos and our confusion. We don't want to be groomed and smart; we want to slob out and be ourselves. We don't want to feel the fear and do it anyway; we want to feel the fear and wimp out. We don't want chicken soup for the soul; we want a nice cup of tea. And we never, ever want to get in touch with anything inner – child, dolphin, biscuit, fear, anger, parent, heart space. We want fast food and decent television. We want to be ineffective, slow, incompetent, meek and idle. We want to rule the world but in a small way.

We want to stop right where we are and not have to improve, be perfect, get better, be part of any process, talk about our trauma. We are doing fine thank you just the way we are. We truly want to be ineffective. We have seen the damage being effective does – wars, pollution, decay, disease, death, famine, politics, supermarkets, lycra, email and air miles – and we don't want to walk that road. However, neither do we want to be Zen, enlightened, pure, spiritual, New Age, MBS, transformed, immortal, yogic, vegetarian, slim, de-toxified, irrigated (colonic or otherwise), beautified or transmogrified. We want to be messy, disorganized, ineffective, ineffectual, slow, late, scruffy, flabby and apathetic. Good luck with it.